Makerspace Careers™

CAREERS IN
ELECTRONICS

TRACY BROWN HAMILTON

Rosen
YA™

New York

For Caroline Bourgeot

Published in 2020 by The Rosen Publishing Group, Inc.
29 East 21st Street, New York, NY 10010

First Edition

Library of Congress Cataloging-in-Publication Data

Names: Hamilton, Tracy Brown, author.
Title: Careers in electronics / Tracy Brown Hamilton.
Description: First edition. | New York, NY: Rosen Publishing, 2020.
| Series: Makerspace careers | Includes bibliographical references
and index. | Audience: Grades 7–12.
Identifiers: LCCN 2018047083| ISBN 9781508188018 (library
bound) | ISBN 9781508188001 (pbk.)
Subjects: LCSH: Electronics—Vocational guidance—Juvenile literature.
Classification: LCC TK7845 .H36 2020 | DDC 621.381023—dc23
LC record available at https://lccn.loc.gov/2018047083

Manufactured in China

CONTENTS

INTRODUCTION

Imagine a learning environment—be it in your school, public library, community center, or other public space—in which you have access to various tools for exploring and working together with others to create something. A makerspace is just that: a place where anyone of any age can have access to hands-on learning tools, cutting-edge technology such as 3D printers, and more low-tech materials like building blocks. At a makerspace, anyone can gain experience in anything from robotics to coding to woodworking—and, of course, electronics.

Makerspaces can help prepare you for a future career in electronics, among other fields, by providing a means for you to gain knowledge and experience in science, technology, engineering, and math (STEM). Beyond educational value, some entrepreneurs have used makerspaces as a sort of platform for developing and creating products and services. Get ready to explore some of the success stories that have makerspace roots.

A makerspace is similar to other social groups with a hobby-related focus, such as a reading group or an arts-and-crafts club. The so-called maker movement—from which makerspace culture comes—is, according to John J. Burke, author of *Makerspaces: A Practical Guide*

A makerspace is the perfect environment to experiment and learn about electronics in a hands-on way while spending time with people who share your curiosity.

for Librarians, "the surge of interest in creating physical items with digital tools and Internet-shared plans and techniques."

Members of makerspaces participate in various creative projects, including but not limited to the following:

- Cardboard construction
- Prototyping
- Woodworking
- Electronics
- Robotics

- Digital fabrication
- Building bicycles and kinetic machines
- Textiles and sewing

Organizing a makerspace requires a public space, materials and tools for projects, and often an expert—a makerspace teacher to guide members in executing their creative vision. More than just a space, a makerspace—particularly for students—is an educational approach based on the philosophy that rather than using technology to entertain, communicate, or just as a distraction, students can use it to be creative. A makerspace is where students (and adults alike) can express their curiosity, explore their own interests, and have access to the tools to develop their ideas into tangible objects.

If you're interested in a career in electronics—a broad field that includes everything from electrician to aerospace engineer—a makerspace is a great opportunity to become familiar with using technical equipment, tinkering around with electronics and circuits, repairing broken electronics, and using other tools like soldering irons and power drills.

Having hands-on experience and confidence with electronics and electronics-related topics will give you an edge later in life as you pursue further education and a successful career.

The following information explores more deeply how makerspaces operate and what the benefits are, specifically focused on setting you on the path to a satisfying career in electronics. It covers how to find a local makerspace and how to go about creating your own if one doesn't already exist. You'll learn about various types of jobs that fall under the category of electronics, as well as the various educational paths you can follow to find a satisfying career.

CHAPTER ONE

WHAT IS A MAKERSPACE, AND HOW CAN I BENEFIT FROM ONE?

Collaboration, community formation, and group learning while creating something new in a single space are at the core of the so-called maker movement. It is a phenomenon that is growing worldwide. And more and more, the movement is involving young people. According to the New Media Consortium's *Horizon Report*, "Makerspaces are expected to be increasingly adopted by schools in one year's time or less to make use of mobile learning and cultivate environments where students take ownership of their education by doing and creating."

The maker movement is a social movement with a creative and community focus, and the benefits of hands-on learning have made makerspaces increasingly popular in schools and public libraries. In 2009, then-president Barack Obama launched his Educate to Innovate campaign, supporting and encouraging making experiences for students. In an address to the National Academy of Sciences, Obama said, "I want us all to think about new and creative ways to engage young people in science and engineering, whether it's science festivals, robotics competitions, fairs that encourage young people to create and build

Working in a makerspace helps prepare you to think in a more innovative, experimental way than learning from a textbook alone does.

and invent—to be makers of things, not just consumers of things." The approach encourages innovation and creativity, in school and beyond.

A BRIEF HISTORY OF MAKERSPACE CULTURE

So how did this all get started? The notion of collaboration, especially with creative tasks—be it flower arranging or woodworking—is not new. But the makerspace culture grew out of a particular do-it-yourself culture. A 2014 article in the *Christian Science Monitor* by Noelle Swan describes the movement as "a new industrial revolution—combining the spirit of the old shop class with modern tech in community 'Do It Yourself' spaces."

As technology and modernity move people further away from working with their own hands—to repair or create—people are now feeling a desire to be more in touch with the physical world, according to Matthew Crawford, author of *Shop Class as Soulcraft*. Returning to the idea of interacting with the world in a hands-on, curious way—to combine "doing" with "thinking"—has gained worldwide appeal. Rather than encourage more academically successful students to focus on books and steer them away from manual tasks, such as small motor repair and woodworking, the maker movement emphasizes the value of both kinds of work for all students, enabling them to have ideas and then also to bring those ideas to life.

John Spencer, former classroom teacher and now author and producer of online project-based learning and makerspace courses, says the makerspace movement is needed because the demands on students and the skills they will require in the future are shifting.

Spencer told Jennifer Gonzalez of the *Cult of Pedagogy* blog:

> There was a time when you could follow the formula: Work hard at school, go to college, and climb a corporate ladder. But because of the complex global economy, because of the creative economy, the information economy, our students are going to have to navigate a maze. The ladder is now a maze. And because it's a maze, what do they need in order to navigate that? They need to be able to engage in iterative thinking, creative thinking, critical thinking, they need to know how to pivot, how to change, how to revise, how to persevere. They need to solve complex problems. They need to think divergently. All of those are involved in that maker mindset.

WHO CAN JOIN A MAKERSPACE, AND WHAT CAN BE LEARNED THERE?

The community and collaborative mission of a makerspace means that anyone—young or old, expert or beginner, artist or scientist, and any gender identity—can belong to one. All you need is curiosity and a desire to experiment and learn about the world and how it works in a hands-on, problem-solving, creative way. If your makerspace is organized through your school, it will likely be limited to students—but that is the only restriction.

The benefits of belonging to and working in makerspaces are many. Belonging to one helps reinforce academic concepts you have learned in classrooms from books and teachers because it enables you to put your intellectual knowledge to real-world use. But there are other benefits. Makerspaces help you learn to work together in

Learning from and working with others—sharing knowledge and coming up with solutions as a team—is a central aspect of makerspaces.

MAKERSPACE ACTIVITIES TO ENCOURAGE LEARNING

You can find many ideas for makerspace projects—particularly related to electronics—online at sites such as Makerspaces.com and Pinterest. Some projects require sophisticated technology to complete, but others can be executed using simple supplies, such as cardboard or building blocks like LEGOs. For example, Matt E. Jenkins—search for GeekGuyMJ on YouTube—offers a way to learn about circuits, electricity, and electronics in a hands-on way. His video shows you how to build a simple circuit with an old pizza box and other basic tools and how to change the path of an electric current to run through different sensors.

Here are a few other sites you can visit to find ideas for projects that will trigger innovation and creative thinking while also reinforcing math and logic skills:

- Makezine: At this website devoted to the makerspace movement, you can find news and project ideas.
- Makerspaces.com: This site offers more than sixty makerspace project ideas of every level, from simple to complex.
- Edutopia: This site offers ideas for makerspace projects at various levels.
- Renovated Learning: If you have a tight budget, this site offers projects that won't be out of reach.

teams, to share and learn from the ideas of others as well as develop confidence in your own innovative ideas and approaches to problem solving. It can make you a more curious thinker, as well as a better communicator.

Experiences in makerspaces help you begin to think like an inventor or entrepreneur, which may lead you to an idea or concept that can improve the world—such as projects that focus on solving environmental problems—or launch your own future business. Challenges in makerspaces can help you learn to be persistent, to keep tinkering with different ideas and approaches until you reach the result you are seeking.

HOW CAN I FIND A MAKERSPACE NEAR ME?

Hands-on experience will be invaluable in preparing you for a career in electronics, no matter which specific career path you decide to pursue. Being familiar with various tools and, of course, applying your math, science, and problem-solving knowledge to a real-world endeavor will make learning more challenging but also more enjoyable and more reinforced.

Finding a makerspace near you will provide a unique and effective opportunity to access tools and technology as well as the expertise of others. So how do you go about finding one?

To start, find out whether your school offers a maker-space program and how you can get involved. If no such

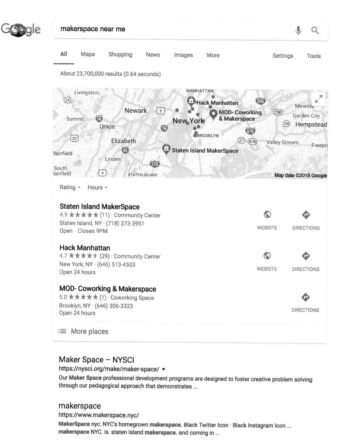

If you are curious about where to find a makerspace near you, there are several apps and websites that can help you locate one.

program exists, check with your local library or community center. If you still have no luck, there are many resources online to help you find a makerspace that fits your interests.

For example, Beauty and the Bolt is a site that maintains an ever-growing list of public makerspaces, libraries with maker resources, and other spaces. Search with your zip code to find a space near you. The Maker Map is a searchable directory that shares information on both makerspaces

THE BASICS OF CREATING AN ELECTRONICS MAKERSPACE

Although the equipment and tools provided in a makerspace can range from the simple to the highly sophisticated, there are some basics, as suggested by Makerspaces.com, that should be priorities when planning and equipping a maker-space for electronic projects.

- An electronics workbench. The workbench is a structure, usually wooden, where makers will actually work. The workbench should be the proper height for those who will be using it and should include a completely level work-ing surface as well as shelves for storing materials and electric outlets. Workbenches can be bought or made by hand with plywood.
- Basic tools. Tools such as breadboards, which are used for building temporary circuits and prototyping, are es-sential. A digital multimeter for measuring electric current, voltage, and resistance is also necessary. Battery hold-ers, test leaders, wire cutters, and screwdrivers are also fundamental tools for working on electronic makerspace projects. Heat guns and soldering irons are also among the recommended tools.
- Electronic components. The following are recommended: switches, for interrupting electrical currents; resistors, which are used to resist the flow of electricity; capacita-tors, which store and discharge electricity; and diodes, which control the direction in which electricity flows.

With this equipment on hand, your makerspace will be set for conducting innovative experiments and working on creative electronics projects. Just be sure to ask for help as you're learning how to use equipment. Working around electricity can be dangerous, and high-temperature tools like soldering irons will burn skin!

and hardware stores. The Maker Directory is a database of resources for makers and makerspaces. In addition, a simple Google search can help you find a makerspace in your area. Social media sites such as Facebook and Instagram can also connect you with makerspace groups in your area or that share projects and experiences virtually.

HOW TO START YOUR OWN MAKERSPACE

If you've searched around for an existing local makerspace but have not had success in finding one, consider starting one on your own—or with a group of fellow students and the support of your school or local library. The main thing you need is an interested community of members, the support of an adult, and a passion for ideas and projects you can work on collaboratively.

Here are the basics of what you will need to launch a successful makerspace.

- Find a space. This is, of course, an essential need. Ideally, it is a space that can be adapted to

If you are interested in joining a makerspace but can't find one in your area, get together with friends and create your own.

various activities. If your school or library does not have a space to spare, consider a space you can use temporarily, such as your school's cafeteria or gymnasium.

- Tools and materials. Keep in mind that you don't need to have an extensive amount of sophisticated, expensive equipment. When just starting, it's best to focus on materials that can be used for a variety of projects rather than a specific one.

- Guidance and support. Although a makerspace is focused on the collaboration of everyone, when working with electronic concepts, it is a good idea to have an adult expert present to guide you as you approach your projects.

CHAPTER TWO

HOW A MAKERSPACE CAN PREPARE YOU FOR AN ELECTRONICS CAREER

A makerspace is a place for creativity and innovation, and the maker culture has grown over the past several years to become a worldwide movement. From a community-focused initiative, it has become recognized as an increasingly valuable educational approach for ensuring that young people are prepared to be the innovators and entrepreneurs of the future. This is especially true for anyone interested in electronics.

An interest in a career in electronics can mean many different things, since the field encompasses so many types of jobs and working environments. Perhaps you see yourself as an electronics engineer, manufacturing electronics equipment. Or perhaps you would rather begin your own business as an electrician. This section will look at the broad definition of electronics and what the aim and focus of the field is.

Although electronics is a broad field that includes a variety of very different types of jobs, belonging to a

Future careers in electronics will require continued innovation and experimentation. Makerspaces can help nurture the inventors of the future.

makerspace will most certainly help you prepare yourself for such a career. The hands-on learning environment of a makerspace can help expand your knowledge of electronics and help you discover what you are most curious about, what kinds of projects you enjoy working on, and eventually what kind of career path you may want to follow.

The pioneers of electronics, with their inventions, experiments, ideas, and research, helped achieve major milestones in the world of technology and communication. Belonging to a makerspace in combination with your schoolwork can keep your interest in learning and your passion for electronics alive and open up the possibility for you to come up with new inventions of your own.

HOW DOES THIS WORK SPECIFICALLY FOR ELECTRONICS?

So, what exactly is the field of electronics, and what types of jobs does it include? In general terms, electronics is a branch of engineering that refers to anything that involves the development and maintenance of devices or systems that deal with electrical circuits—including but not limited to vacuum tubes or semiconductors. The term itself comes from "electron mechanics."

The general field of electronics involves creating new technology—hardware, such as computers or robots—that help solve challenges or improve how people work, play, and live. It is a field that is ripe for innovation, invention, and creative solutions. For example, in 1947, Bell Laboratories developed the transistor, an invention that has had a major impact. The transistor is a device that controls the amount of electrical current that passes through circuit boards. It is a key component to endless modern technical devices on which many rely, including televisions, cell phones, digital cameras, ATM technology, and computers.

The core goal of electronics is to think outside the box to refine the ways in which electronic technologies

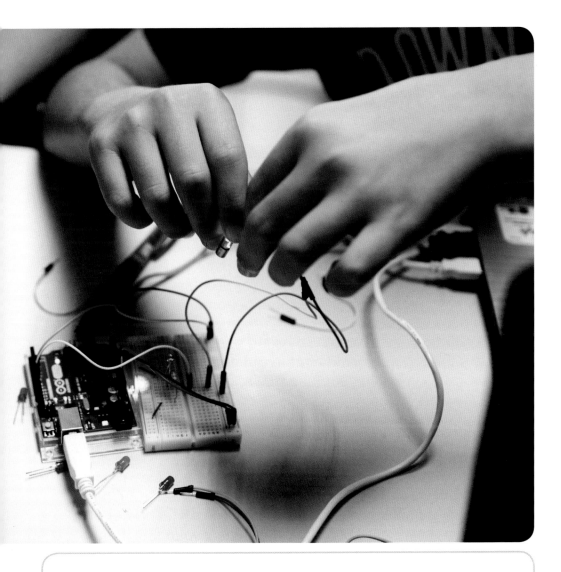

One of the biggest benefits of working in a makerspace is the opportunity to work with actual tools, no matter how basic or advanced.

are used. With a stronger awareness of the importance of environmental protection, for example, there is an increased focus on limiting the damage electronic technologies do to the planet, including pollution, resource

THE POWER OF DESIGN THINKING FOR PROBLEM SOLVING

In traditional educational processes, a teacher transfers knowledge to students through lectures and textbooks and assesses how well the students have retained the knowledge through asking questions and giving homework and tests. This is an effective way to learn theoretical knowledge, but in a makerspace you are able to apply that knowledge to an actual problem that needs to be solved creatively. This goes beyond merely tinkering with tools, since it is more focused on coming up with a solution—it is a method called design thinking, which is used not only in education but also in the corporate world. Companies such as IBM and Fidelity have design labs where employees can seek out ways to innovate and then make prototypes of new products. For example, a design project at the College for Creative Studies in Detroit, Michigan, in which the challenge was to do something to help the homeless population, resulted in the development of the EMPWR coat, a water-resistant jacket that can convert into a sleeping bag. The nonprofit that now makes the coat offers the public the chance to pay for the production of one coat that is then given to a homeless person. This type of innovation is what makerspaces are all about!

consumption, and waste caused by older, no-longer-used hardware.

A makerspace focusing on engineering and electronics will give you an opportunity to experiment safely with wiring,

A makerspace—similar to a hackerspace and other community-based learning environments of different names—brings people with similar interests and ideas together.

soldering, and programming. Since most makerspaces are focused on science, technology, engineering, and math—all of which relate strongly to the field of electronics—you will have the chance to reinforce your knowledge in these areas by applying them to projects or experimenting with ways in which you think electronic technologies can work differently or better.

MAKERSPACE, HACKERSPACE, TECHSHOP, AND FABLAB: WHAT IS THE DIFFERENCE?

You may have encountered other terms for similar initiatives to a makerspace, including hackerspace, TechShop, and FabLab. Although these are all similar, there are some differences.

The hackerspace is a concept born in Europe. One of the first hackerspaces was launched by German programmers in the mid-1990s. The idea was to gather programmers together in one physical space. Today, hackerspaces are typically community-based, nonprofit spaces where people gather to share a similar interest in computers, technology, and science—all very relevant to a career in electronics.

A TechShop is a trademarked name, the first of which opened in California in 2006. The idea was to enable access to members, who paid a fee, to industrial equipment to work on projects that involved work such as woodworking, machining, welding, and sewing.

A FabLab is also a trademarked name, and the concept was the brainchild of Neil Gershenfeld of the Massachusetts Institute of Technology in 2005. A FabLab—which stands for "fabrication laboratory"—is usually equipped with equipment to be used for digital modeling and fabrication, which entails 3D printing and computer-based design.

INCORPORATING MAKERSPACE EXPERIENCE WITH EDUCATION

Even when you have a strong knowledge of and interest in a certain subject—such as electronics—without access to hands-on experience with technology, learning can be less enjoyable and less stimulating. A makerspace combined with classroom education gives students an opportunity to learn through hands-on creation and collaboration, offering you the best way to maintain your interest and passion and develop your practical skills. These are skills that will go beyond teaching you existing electronics concepts and will let you develop your own ideas.

According to Matthew Lynch, writing for the Tech Edvocate, makerspaces are the key to innovation:

> Makerspaces are creative spaces located in communities, schools, and public and academic libraries. These areas are designed to engage participants in hands-on activities that teach twenty-first-century skills. The emphasis in makerspaces is placed upon educating students in STEAM (science, technology, engineering, art and mathematics) subjects as well as digital and information literacy.

A makerspace is so valuable in education because it enables students to explore skills beyond the actual academic subject. These include:

- Self-directed learning. In a makerspace, you are in control. You can explore whatever is of interest to you relating to electronics.
- Creativity. The sky is the limit. Whether it is in choosing a project to pursue or solving a problem you encounter on the way, creative thinking is key to a makerspace environment.
- Confidence. There's no right or wrong in a makerspace, and no silly questions or ideas.

- Comfort with failure. The name of the makerspace game is experimentation. If at first your idea does not succeed, seek out a new possible solution and persevere.
- Focus. Just sitting and reading a book or listening to a lecture is not always the best way to grab someone's attention and help him or her learn. In a makerspace, you can actively focus on a problem and engage hands on with an experiment.
- Self-expression and the ability to collaborate. Because of the community focus and working-in-teams nature of a makerspace, you will learn to express your ideas and respect those of others to come to an agreement.

Makerspaces in education are growing rapidly in popularity, and their value in helping prepare students to help improve the world and how we live in it in the future is part of a major shift in how education is approached in the twenty-first century. This applies in particular to electronics because of all the various ways the field impacts how we live, what we discover, how we communicate, how we play, how we work, and so on.

CHAPTER THREE

ELECTRONICS AS A CAREER: WHAT ARE SOME OF THE CHOICES?

Electronics as a career and field of study, as previously stated, is a very broad field that encompasses several different types of jobs. *Merriam-Webster* defines "electronics" as "a branch of physics that deals with the emission, behavior, and effects of electrons (as in electron tubes and transistors) and with electronic devices."

Careers ranging from automotive electronics to aerospace engineers and from computer consultants to residential electricians all fall under the umbrella of electronics. Each career requires different types of educational preparation to enter—and each is responsible for different tasks in different environments—but they all begin with a need for a curious mind and an interest in and understanding of electricity.

For each of these careers, participating in a makerspace project to hone your skills and general knowledge, as well as to gain experience working with various tools and equipment and to share knowledge in a collaborative environment, will help prepare you for success in the job of your choosing.

An interest in the field of electronics offers you a variety of options as far as where and what type of work you can do.

ELECTRICAL ENGINEER

An electronics engineer is tasked with carrying out the design, development, and research related to electrical systems. These systems include everything from the design of a simple lamp to complex projects like developing space shuttle technologies. Jobs in this category can range from military weaponry development to commercial product design.

According to the Bureau of Labor Statistics, in 2017 the average annual salary for this type of work was $95,060.

THE FUTURE OF ELECTRONICS CAREERS

Technology is all about change. The way we use technology in our lives, the way technology is designed, and new developments make the field of electronics an ever-changing one—which is part of what makes it so innovative and exciting. Keeping up with these changes and evolutions and continuously thinking about ways in which existing technology and electric systems can be improved are key functions of an electrician or engineer. Colin Simpson, an electronics professional and dean of the Centre for Continuous Learning at George Brown College in Toronto, Canada, concurs in an interview with Trade Schools, Colleges and Universities. "Technology is evolving at breakneck speed," he says, "and it is crucial that people in the field of electronics are able to adapt to these changes." Although it's not easy to predict the future with certainty, Simpson suggests some technology shifts that all members of the electronics field should see as signs of changes to come. Among them are robotics and automation, which are changing industrial processes, and near-field communication, used to create short-range wireless networks.

The highest-paying industries include scientific research, the federal government, and the aerospace industry.

An electrical engineer can expect to work together with people in areas such as engineering, product development, implementation, and international contract manufacturing partners.

ELECTRONICS TECHNICIAN

An electronics technician is responsible for designing, testing, and building various types of electronic equipment. Such equipment can be applied to anything from communication to navigation to medicine.

The Bureau of Labor Statistics placed the average annual salary for this field at around $63,660 in 2017. Top earners work in industries such as the oil and gas extraction industry and waste treatment and disposal.

The installation and inspection of equipment are also the responsibility of an electronics technician, which can

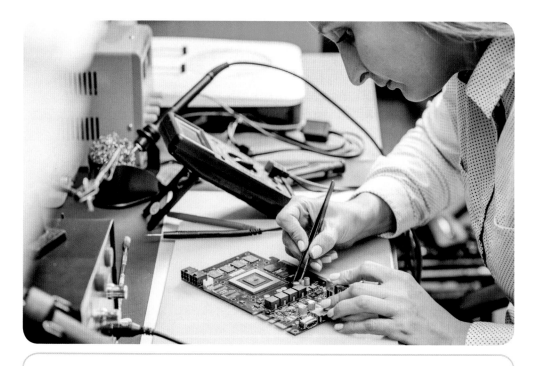

Depending on the specific type of career within the field of electronics you choose, your educational requirements and salary expectations will differ.

include anything from air-conditioning and heating systems to power tools and other machinery. The job requires an extensive knowledge of electronics and electronic equipment.

ELECTRONICS ENGINEER

An electronics engineer designs, develops, and tests parts, devices, systems, and equipment that at least in part rely on electricity as a source of power, including capacitors, diodes, resistors, and transistors. This includes a broad range of industries, including acoustics, military defense, medical instruments and technologies, mobile phone technology, radio and satellite communication, and robotics. According to the Bureau of Labor Statistics, the average annual salary for this field is $97,970 per year, or $47.10 per hour.

An electronics engineer needs to have not only technical knowledge but interpersonal and communication skills, since he or she may be involved in working with clients and other team members on complex projects. Developing and following procedures and ensuring that safety requirements are met also falls on the shoulders of an electronics engineer.

INFORMATION TECHNOLOGY (IT) CONSULTANT

An IT consultant wears many hats. He or she works with companies and organizations to ensure IT systems are properly installed, maintained, and protected from security issues and other malfunctions. The work entails everything from offering advice on technical solutions and the best technologies for the task at hand to ensuring employees work with the installed technologies with efficiency and ease. IT consultants are also responsible for making sure technical processes, products, and systems are working at full capacity to increase business efficiency and success.

As in any consulting capacity, beyond knowledge of technology and computer systems, success depends on communication skills, the ability to promote yourself as a consultant, and the capacity to establish trust with clients by listening to their concerns and finding the right solutions.

AEROSPACE ENGINEER

An aerospace engineer works on projects relating to technology that supports flight. This can mean anything from jet planes to spacecraft, making it a very exciting and demanding field. In 2017, according to the Bureau of Labor Statistics, the average annual salary for this field was $110,570 per year.

The job entails researching or developing materials to be used in the construction of aircraft or the equipment used to shoot missiles or rockets. The job requires expertise in mechanics, thermodynamics, robotics, and aerodynamics.

This is a very specialized industry, which means direct duties or tasks will vary depending on the field in which you work.

With a job in the electronics field, you can find yourself working on exciting and complex problems, finding solutions to everything, even getting rockets into space.

ELECTRONICS INSTALLATION AND REPAIR

Field technicians are charged with performing routine maintenance where electronic equipment is located. As an electronics installer, it is your job to maintain and upgrade older equipment with new devices for controlling operations and installing new systems. You may work on surveillance, security, communications, and navigation systems.

The Bureau of Labor Statistics states that these workers earn an average hourly salary of $24.62 and an annual salary of $51,210.

LAUNCHING A BUSINESS THROUGH MAKERSPACES

Although schools create makerspaces with the purpose of teaching students about subjects like robotics and science, technology, electronics, and math (STEM) in a more meaningful and hands-on manner, there have also been many instances in which makers have created products in a makerspace environment that have gone on to become successful businesses.

One example is a smartwatch called the Pebble—a watch that can deliver messages from smartphones and Android devices—which was the brainchild of inventor Eric Migicovsky and has its roots as a prototype project in a TechShop.

Because makerspaces give entrepreneurs access to the industrial tools and equipment needed to create prototypes of their inventions—such as 3D printers and laser cutters—these spaces are invaluable for makers who would otherwise not be able to get their hands on these resources. But equally valuable for entrepreneurs is the shared knowledge and collaboration across the makerspace community.

Once a product prototype is developed, many entrepreneurs pursue nontraditional funding paths to bring their invention to market. The Pebble watch, for example, was funded through a Kickstarter campaign—a funding platform for creative projects. Makerspaces and alternative funding methods are providing more and more entrepreneurs with the means to experiment with their ideas and bring them to fruition and to start successful businesses.

COMPUTER HARDWARE ENGINEER

The job of a computer hardware engineer is to perform research to support the development, design, and testing of new computer systems. Hardware means the actual physical equipment used in computing, versus the software programs that run on or with the support of this equipment. That means processors, memory devices, networks, routers, and so on. The Bureau of Labor Statistics estimates that in 2017 the annual salary of such engineers was $100,920.

Computer hardware engineers do often work together with software engineers to ensure the software will run correctly. They also work closely with entities such as the automobile or medical industries to develop hardware specific to the needs of those fields.

ELECTRICIAN

An electrician is responsible for installing and maintaining the electrical

The field of electronics is a steady one because electricity is used in almost every aspect of our lives.

power, communications, and lighting systems in buildings. These systems—which power the lighting, appliances, and so on that we depend on at work and at home—are installed during the construction of new structures but then need to be repaired and maintained after that. To do this, electricians have to be able to read blueprints, which map out the electrical wiring in a building. According to the Bureau of Labor Statistics, the average salary for an electrician in 2017 was $37.39 per hour, or $77,770 per year. The job outlook for electricians is generally good and steady since the need for this type of job remains consistent.

CHAPTER FOUR

PREPARING FOR A CAREER IN ELECTRONICS WITHOUT A FOUR-YEAR DEGREE

Although some careers in electronics, such as aerospace engineer, will require advanced education, not all areas of this field do. Not everyone wants to go to a four-year college or university, and some prefer to begin on-the-job training and launch their careers as soon as possible. With many electronics careers, this is possible.

Apprenticeship programs, in which you are trained on the job, as well as certification programs that test and confirm skills in key areas are sufficient if you want to pursue a career as an electrician or technician, for example. Keep in mind, however, that a high school diploma or equivalent is required.

HOW TO PREPARE DURING MIDDLE SCHOOL AND HIGH SCHOOL

Although you may think you have to wait until you graduate from high school to start taking steps to prepare for your

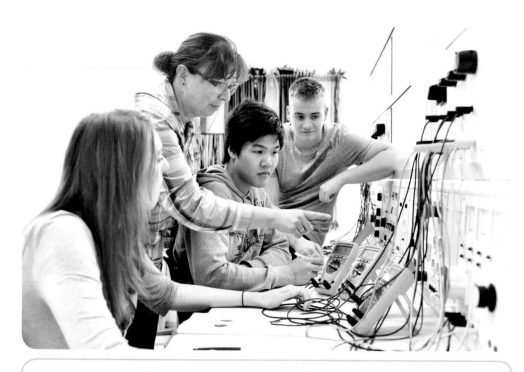

It's never too early to start working on your future career goals. Honing skills that will prepare you for success later is possible no matter where you are in your education.

career, there are several ways—other than graduating—that you can advance your chances for career success while in high school. There are, for example, courses to take and skills you should hone to help set you up for success after you receive your high school diploma. And, of course, participating in a makerspace can help you further develop and hone the skills that you will need for a career in electronics.

If you are interested in electronics, you probably already have a passion and competence in subjects such as math and science. If you are interested in a career as an electrician or electrical technician, consider

A BRIEF HISTORY OF THE FIELD OF ELECTRONICS

As you learn more about the world of electronics, it is important to know where it all started. Key discoveries in electronics, all of which helped make possible modern electrical technologies, can be traced back to 600 BCE, when Greek philosopher Thales of Miletus discovered static electricity. The term "electricity" was coined in 1600 CE by English physician, physicist, and natural philosopher William Gilbert.

The field has plenty of other key players to thank, whose curiosity and experimentation led to major breakthroughs in electronics:

- **Francis Hauksbee:** Although he was not the first to create

Englishman William Gilbert helped lay the groundwork for modern-day electronics innovations.

(*continued on the next page*)

(*continued from the previous page*)

an electrostatic generator—a generator that produces static electricity—Hauksbee created a stir in 1705 when he used his device to make a glass ball glow as he spun it and rubbed in with his hand.

- Benjamin Franklin: In 1752, this American scientist proved the electrical nature of lightning by flying a kite in a thunderstorm.
- Francis Ronalds: In 1816, this English inventor built the first working electric telegraph.
- Samuel Morse: This American inventor developed and patented a recording electric telegraph in 1837. He later developed Morse code.
- Alexander Graham Bell: This Scottish inventor patented the telephone in 1876.
- Konrad Zuse: This German engineer was the developer of the first programmable computer.

Teams of engineers were responsible for other major firsts in electronics, including the first TV broadcast experiment in the United States in 1928 and the first nuclear power plant in the country, which appeared in 1951.

other skills that will be key in your work, such as business, communication, critical thinking, customer service, and troubleshooting. If possible, consider working in a hardware store or other related business, which will help you develop communication and customer-service skills, as well as give you the opportunity to deepen your knowledge of the tools and equipment that are used by electricians or technicians.

Working in a makerspace in addition to taking business, math, and science courses can significantly assist you in developing the skills you need. Working in collaboration with a team of other makers will help you become a better communicator and troubleshooter. The opportunity to work with different tools and equipment will give you an edge in real-world experience and give you the chance to think on your feet to come up with solutions to issues in a real situation, rather than a hypothetical one in a textbook.

HOW TO CHOOSE THE RIGHT EDUCATION PATH

After high school, there are various educational paths— besides the four-year college path—you can follow. The basic requirements before you get started are that you are at least eighteen years old, have earned your high school diploma or equivalent, and can pass an aptitude test— which covers subjects such as algebra, electrical concepts, process and signal flow, and electrical sequences. Most often, it's required that you pass a substance abuse test.

Most electricians follow an apprenticeship that usually runs for four to five years. Apprentices get technical training (usually at least 114 hours) and must complete 2,000 hours of on-the-job training. Electrical technicians, however, usually pursue a two-year associate's degree at a vocational school or community college in areas such as electrical technology or electrical and computer engineering technology. In some cases, earning a certificate in an accredited program is sufficient.

The technical training for electricians, which takes place in a classroom environment, covers everything from electrical theory to blueprint reading, math, electrical code requirements, safety measures, and even first aid. Some courses offer specialized training, such as working with fire-alarm systems or elevators.

Once the apprenticeship is completed, you are qualified to work independently, although each state does have its own licensing requirements. These licensing tests include questions relating to the national electrical code as well as state and local codes. You can learn about these by contacting the electrical licensing board in your region or state. As safety and electrical codes change over time, additional continuing education courses may be required to ensure you are up-to-date.

HOW TO GET AN APPRENTICESHIP

Finding an apprenticeship is a required step to becoming an electrician. There are three main apprenticeship programs in the United States that provide paid, on-the-job training for future electricians. More information about them is available at the Electrician Apprentice Headquarters website.

The International Brotherhood of Electrical Workers Apprenticeship Program is an apprenticeship program organized by the International Brotherhood of Electrical Workers and the National Electrical Contractors Association. The program offers several training tracks, including

Many people entering the field of electronics begin by participating in apprenticeship programs, learning the profession while working under an expert's guidance.

outside lineman, inside wireman, sound and communication technicians, and residential wireman.

The Independent Electrical Contractors (IEC) is an independent (nonunion) trade association. Its chapters offer more than fifty training centers across the United States and train approximately ten thousand apprentices annually. The IEC offers training programs for electrical apprentices, which take four years to complete and require 8,000 hours of on-the-job training plus 576 hours of instruction. It also offers apprenticeships for residential electrical

DECIDING WHETHER TO JOIN A UNION

A union is an organization that has members who are working in the same profession. The purpose of a union is to offer protection to workers and ensure they are able to negotiate with managers on any issues pertaining to the quality of their work life. The International Brotherhood of Electrical Workers (IBEW) is the largest electrician's union in the United States. In 2012, electricians belonged to unions at a higher percentage than any other profession in the nation.

So what are the benefits of being in a union? Following are some of the securities a union can help you achieve as an electrician:

- Better salary: According to the IBEW, union workers earn approximately 15 percent more than their non-union counterparts.
- Benefits: Union workers are better able to negotiate benefits, including health care, paid holidays, sick pay, and overtime pay.
- Job security: When you belong to a union, your job is better protected. You cannot be fired without warning or reason, nor can you be demoted without cause.
- An activist role: Unions are run democratically by workers and afford you a platform to be heard by management in all subjects relating to your work life.

specialists, which can be completed in two or three years and require 4,000 hours of on-the-job training and 288 hours of instruction.

Part of the Associated Builders and Contractors (ABC)—a national construction trade association—the ABC Electrical Apprenticeship program has seventy chapters across the United States and approximately twenty-one thousand members nationwide. The apprenticeships usually take four years to complete and require 144 hours of instruction each year to complete.

CERTIFICATE PROGRAMS AND TWO-YEAR DEGREES

Anyone interested in pursuing a career as an electrical technician can choose to follow a certificate program or earn a two-year degree at a vocational school or community college. The latter option provides more of a foundation and more career options. The following describes three options and how they prepare you for your career.

- Electrical or maintenance certificate: This certificate program provides a foundation in electrical and maintenance subjects. The programs can be followed online or on a campus and usually take from one to two years to complete. The courses followed include industrial wiring, mechanical installation, and power tool use.

There are many academic options for pursuing a career in electronics, and the type of degree required also varies depending on your career goal.

- Associate's degree in applied science in electrical technology: This degree, which takes two years to complete full time, provides students both academic and hands-on study dealing with electrical devices and circuits. Subjects covered include advanced electricity and industrial electronics, automation, rotational machinery, and motors and controls.

- Associate's degree in applied science in electrical and computer engineering technology: This two-year program prepares students for careers as engineering technicians. It is also possible to choose a specialization in electronics. Subjects covered include circuit analysis, digital systems, electronics, and electromechanical devices. Upon completing the associate's degree, you may begin working professionally or consider pursuing a bachelor's degree in a related subject.

CHAPTER FIVE

PREPARING FOR A CAREER IN ELECTRONICS WITH A HIGHER-EDUCATION DEGREE

Different careers in the field of electronics require varying levels of education and training. You can begin working in some jobs—such as electrician and electrical technician—with a high school degree or equivalent and an apprenticeship to provide on-the-job training along with additional certifications to show your expertise.

Other jobs, however, require further education, including four-year-degrees (called bachelor's degrees) or even additional degrees, such as a master's degree or even a doctorate, also known as a PhD. Examples include engineering jobs and IT consultant jobs. Understanding the educational path you will need to follow is an important step in planning your future. Knowing which programs of study exist in the United States and which degree will best prepare you for the type of career you want—as well as which schools offer the best degrees in those subject areas—will help make your decision about where to

Although not everyone wants—or needs—to go to college, it is a requirement for some careers. Research carefully to find the right school and program to meet your goals.

continue your education after high school clearer. During junior high or high school, you can do a lot to prepare for your future academic path after graduation.

HOW TO PREPARE DURING HIGH SCHOOL

There are several ways—in addition to graduating—that you can advance your chances for career success while in high school. For a career in electronics—especially if it is your plan to pursue a university degree in a related area after high school—it is fundamental that you take as many courses as you can (and at as high a level as you can) in subjects like math, science, and technology. In math, you will be expected to have taken subjects like algebra, geometry, probability and statistics, and calculus. In science, be sure to take courses in areas such as physical science, biology, chemistry, and physics.

Other subjects that you might not consider as valuable for a career in electronics involve communication and writing skills. For that reason, while you may be tempted to focus solely on science and math, keep in mind that you should also be taking English, composition and writing, and other communication-focused classes. And, of course, hands-on experience with tools, working in teams, and finding solutions to real-world problems while working in a makerspace will give you invaluable experience—more so than what you can learn theoretically from a textbook.

WHAT COLLEGE MAJORS TO CONSIDER FOR A CAREER IN ELECTRONICS

Depending on what kind of electronics-based work you want to do in the future, there are several relevant degree programs you can follow to prepare you. Generally, electronics majors focus

their studies on subjects like engineering, computers, and math. Electrical engineering degrees provide students a

There are so many choices of programs and colleges offering degrees to prepare you for an electronics career. Consider your options carefully!

background to prepare them for careers in fields such as telecommunication and consumer electronics.

Electronics degree programs teach skills such as testing electrical equipment and assessing and solving technical issues. These degree programs require a solid understanding of math (mainly calculus) and physics. Lab experience will involve working with electrical equipment, including linear circuits and microprocessors.

A bachelor's degree in electrical engineering will usually take four years to complete as a full-time student. Upon earning the degree, a graduate will be prepared for entry-level positions such as control engineers (who make electrical systems work efficiently), design engineers (who work on prototyping products and systems to solve problems), and electrical engineers (who design and develop new electrical equipment).

After completing a bachelor's degree, you may choose to continue with your education before seeking employment or get some work experience before returning to school. Master's and PhD degrees in electrical engineering can better prepare you for higher-level jobs in your field.

SCHOOLS OFFERING ELECTRONICS-RELATED DEGREE PROGRAMS

Deciding where to go to college is a difficult undertaking. There are many considerations to mull over, including where you want to live, whether you want to study full time or work your way through school, whether you want to be

WHEN TO CONSIDER A PHD IN ELECTRICAL ENGINEERING

For most people seeking a career in electronics, a PhD, or doctoral degree, is not necessary. In some cases, however—such as if your goal is to teach electronics in a college or university—it will be a requirement. If your intention is to work in the field rather than follow an academic career, the PhD on its own will still not fulfill the requirements to begin working. The certifications and on-the-job training hours will still need to be met before you can begin your career. So committing the hours and money to earning a PhD is probably only necessary if your ultimate goal is a career in academics.

on campus or study through an online degree program, and, of course, what kind of financial support you can qualify for in order to help fund your education.

Another consideration to keep in mind is what the value of your degree will be upon graduation. While any advanced education will help prepare you for a job in your field of interest or study, there are schools that are specifically known for having excellent programs with solid reputations for training top students who become top members of their professional fields. These schools will be quite competitive, which is why it is so important to gain all the extra experience and education that you can before applying to college.

MAKE THE SUMMER COUNT WITH A CAREER-PREPARATION PROGRAM

Getting into college is a competitive process, and it can be daunting, to say the least. Trying to stand out from the many other applicants—particularly if you are aiming for some of the top-ranked programs in the United States—is challenging. It is unfortunately not enough to have earned good grades in high school. The more you can do to prepare yourself, the better. Finding a summer job that relates in some way to the career path you want to pursue is one way to show additional knowledge, drive, and experience on your résumé and college application. Experience with a makerspace is obviously another great way to gain this extra edge when applying to college. Another possibility, however, is to take part in a summer career program.

Envision is an organization that offers programs in science, technology, engineering, and math (STEM) for third through twelfth graders, as well as programs focusing on leadership and innovation—both equally important for a successful career in electronics. Many colleges and universities also offer summer courses for high school students that provide additional academic experience and knowledge, as well as a sense of the college life experience. Search online for such programs or speak to your guidance counselor at school to see if he or she can help find one that is right for you.

Each year, *U.S. News & World Report* publishes a list of the top schools in a particular field of study. For electrical, electronic, and communication engineering programs, the following schools ranked highest in the United States in 2018:

1. Massachusetts Institute of Technology, Cambridge, Massachusetts
2. Stanford University, Stanford, California
3. University of California, Berkeley, Berkeley, California
4. University of Illinois, Urbana-Champaign, Urbana, Illinois
5. California Institute of Technology, Pasadena, California
6. Georgia Institute of Technology, Atlanta, Georgia
7. University of Michigan, Ann Arbor, Ann Arbor, Michigan
8. Carnegie Mellon University, Pittsburgh, Pennsylvania
9. Cornell University, Ithaca, New York
10. Princeton University, Princeton, New Jersey
11. Purdue University, West Lafayette, Indiana
12. University of Texas, Austin, Austin, Texas

It is definitely not necessary for you to go to a top school in the country in order to succeed in your future career, and it is worth looking at the different programs available and considering their strengths and weaknesses. Perhaps there's a school that has a particular specialization in the area you are most interested in, such as aerospace engineering, or perhaps you learn best in an environment with a smaller student population or higher instructor-to-student ratio. While rankings are informative, it is your individual preferences and needs that should drive your decision-making process when considering college applications.

CONSIDERING ONLINE LEARNING

Many schools offer online degree programs in various subjects, including electronics. One benefit of online programs is that participants need not relocate. They can stay in their own city or town while completing their studies online from an institution in another state or region.

Admissions requirements to such programs are the same as campus-based programs—and are competitive as well. While course work can be completed online, some programs require students to complete an internship. In many cases, if you are already working as an engineer, your

Online programs are becoming increasingly available and respected, and they are a great alternative if relocating for school or studying full time on campus is difficult.

work experience will be counted toward your degree requirements.

According to BestColleges.com, the following schools offer the top online programs in electrical engineering:

1. Clemson University, Clemson, South Carolina
2. Arizona State University, Tempe, Tempe, Arizona
3. University of North Dakota, Grand Forks, North Dakota
4. Stony Brook University, Stony Brook, New York
5. Morgan State University, Baltimore, Maryland

CHAPTER SIX

PREPARING FOR YOUR CAREER

Thinking about what kind of job you want to have in the future can be intimidating because there are so many choices to consider. If your interest in subjects such as science and math have already made it obvious to you that you want to work in the field of electronics, you are well on your way to knowing what you want to do in your career—but there are still many choices to make and options to think about.

It's also perfectly OK if you are still not sure specifically what you want to do. There are many things to consider as you make your career choice, particularly as you start seriously considering the training track required—be it an apprenticeship or a PhD—to achieve your goal.

The undeniable benefit of a makerspace is that it provides a chance to get firsthand experience in what it is like to apply your knowledge to actual tinkering, experimenting, troubleshooting, problem solving, and creating, all while

As you start to visualize your future profession, keep in mind other factors that account for work-life balance, such as the environment you want to work in.

working together with a team of other students with a similar passion for electronics.

There are many types of questions you can ask yourself in order to help you think about where you really want to see yourself in the future, what you want your work life to be, in what environment you want to work, and in what capacity. These are all difficult questions, but considering them carefully can help you ensure you have a deeper understanding of what you want and how to get there.

CONSIDERING WHERE AND HOW YOU WANT TO WORK

In a field as broad as electronics, it can be difficult to narrow your choices down to a specific area. Think about what kind of environment you want to work in: do you see yourself doing research and development or working in the field? Do you see yourself working for yourself or for a large corporation? How much flexibility do you want? What kinds of colleagues would you like to work with, and what kind of work culture would you like?

DO YOU HAVE WHAT IT TAKES TO BE AN ELECTRICIAN?

If you are considering a future as an electrician, you will need more than just an understanding of how electricity and electrical systems work. There are other personal characteristics that will come into play. For example, given that you will be working with lots of different-colored wires, one requirement is that you have excellent color vision. But there are other factors to consider, and one useful resource is an online quiz provided by the Balance Careers website. The quiz poses the question: do you have what it takes to be an electrician? And it includes questions such as "Picture yourself walking along a balance beam. How does it go?" and "Are you good at picking up small objects and using your fingers?"

To begin to answer these questions, it's helpful to think outside of the career box and take into account your personality and interests beyond the job you see yourself having later in life. For example, think about what you most enjoy doing outside of school and what it is you like most about those activities. Also think about how you like to approach problems or assignments and how you learn best. Do you like working in teams or solving problems on your own? Maybe you prefer to work with your hands, like to conduct experiments, or are more research focused. Taking these characteristics and preferences into account can help you form a better idea of the best kind of working environment for you.

SEEKING HELP TO FIND THE ANSWERS

How can you get a sense of whether you will love your career choice before you have put in the educational, financial, and time commitment required to pursue it? You don't want to find yourself halfway through an electrical engineering degree program before realizing it's not what you want. Fortunately, there are lots of ways—including by participating in a makerspace—that you can get experience and insight into an electrical career, no matter your age or grade. Here are a few suggestions:

- Take a career assessment test. These tests, many of which are available online, can help you understand what type of career best suits you.
- Talk with professionals already working in the field.

Career planning can be a very complicated and confusing process, but don't get overwhelmed. There are plenty of tools, such as assessment tests, and experts to help you make decisions.

In many makerspace environments—although not all—a skilled adult will be available to support you. Talk with that person about what he or she likes about his or her work, what a typical day is like, and what challenges he or she faces. Talk to as many people as you can—such as a local electrician, for example—to get a better sense of what the job is actually like.

- Job shadow a professional in the electronics field. It may be possible to join an electronics professional in his or her workplace to get a sense of what the atmosphere is like, the hours, the flexibility, and his or her working relationship with colleagues.

THINKING HOLISTICALLY ABOUT WORK AND LIFE

You might hear a lot of adults talking about work-life balance. In simple terms, it refers to the way in which your job blends in with the rest of your life and lifestyle and how much your job allows you to have time to take part in other activities, like hobbies, spending time with family, or eating healthfully and getting enough rest.

Companies are becoming increasingly aware of the importance of work-life balance for the health and happiness of their employees. The job site Glassdoor includes a space for employees to rate their experiences with their companies—including electronics companies such as LG and Electronic Arts—on anything from work culture to salary to work-life balance. It's easier and easier to get a glimpse of what it would be like to be working at a particular place—for example, whether you will be expected to work very long hours with little vacation time.

Often when thinking about the future, especially while you are still in school, the focus is on career. But your future will involve many more factors than just the work you do. If you'd like to have a life in which you work a regular nine-to-five type of job, then perhaps life as an oil rig electrician is not for you. If you'd like to own your own business and make your own hours, perhaps working as an independent residential electrician is the best choice. Perhaps you are eager to travel and live many places, or perhaps you see yourself never leaving your hometown. All of these, of course, are far-off choices, but considering them as you begin your career path is a good idea and will better prepare you to be happy, not only with your job but also with how it fits into and supports the rest of your life.

There is also such a thing as school-life balance. With so many requirements, courses to take, and tests to pass, it can be easy to put aside what makes you really inspired and happy: the freedom to experiment, to push up your sleeves and work with your hands, to enjoy learning through doing in the company of others who challenge and push you forward, or to actually apply what you know in a real-world situation. That is the value of a makerspace. Because whatever your future, it will involve experimenting, working with others, and applying your knowledge, and a makerspace will help prepare you for an exciting career in electronics.

apprenticeship Work that can be paid or unpaid and is performed under guidance in order to learn a trade.

associate's degree A two-year college degree that can be earned at a vocational school or community college.

bachelor's degree A four-year college degree that is awarded by a university or college.

blueprint A detailed map showing how a building was constructed and where the electrical systems are within the structure.

circuit The complete path of an electric current.

electrical engineer A person who works on the design, development, and maintenance of electrical products and systems.

electric current An electric current is a flow of electric charge.

FabLab A lab that is similar to a makerspace but focuses on digital modeling and fabrication projects.

hackerspace A community-based, nonprofit space where people gather to share a similar interest in computers, technology, and science.

hands-on experience The act of learning while actually doing, rather than reading theory.

makerspace A working space where people with similar interests come together to work collaboratively on projects.

on-the-job training Training in which a person learns a trade while actually working in it.

robotics The branch of technology that deals with the design, construction, operation, and application of robots.

semiconductors Things that can conduct electricity in some instances but not in others.

soldering A method of joining metals using a heat source.

trade A particular skill-based profession, such as an electrician.

union An organization of people in the same occupation that is focused on securing a high standard of working conditions.

vacuum tubes Sealed glass tubes that reveal the effects of electricity passed through them.

vocational school A type of post–high school learning institution that focuses on teaching a trade.

Associated Builders and Contractors
440 First Street NW, Suite 200
Washington, DC 20001
(202) 595-1505
Website: https://www.abc.org
Facebook and Twitter: @ABCNational
Instagram: @abcnational
This national construction industry trade association rep-
   resents more than twenty-one thousand members.

Association for Computing Machinery
2 Penn Plaza, Suite 701
New York, NY 10121
(212) 869-7440
Website: https://www.acm.org
Facebook: @AssociationforComputingMachinery
Twitter: @TheOfficialACM
This society of computing professionals encourages job
   seekers to get involved in the computer field.

Brilliant Labs
Website: https://www.brilliantlabs.ca/about-us
Facebook: @brilliantlabslabosbrillants
Twitter: @brilliant_labs
This nonprofit hands-on technology and experiential learn-
   ing platform is based in Canada.

Canadian Electrical Contractors Association
41 Maple Street

Uxbridge, ON L9P 1C8
Canada
(416) 491-2414
Website: http://www.ceca.org
Facebook: @Canadian-Electrical-Contractors-Association
This organization represents electrical contractors in Canada at the national level.

Independent Electrical Contractors
4401 Ford Avenue, Suite 1100
Alexandria, VA 22302
(703) 549-7351
Website: https://www.ieci.org
Facebook and Twitter: @IEC.National
Instagram: @iec.national
This national trade association is for merit shop electrical and systems contractors.

International Brotherhood of Electrical Workers
900 Seventh Street NW
Washington, DC 20001
(202) 833-7000
Website: http://www.ibew.org
Facebook: @IBEWFB
Twitter and Pinterest: @ibew
This union has more than 750,000 members in electrical careers and bargains for employment rights, including wages and benefits.

Makerspace for Education
Website: http://www.makerspaceforeducation.com
This site provides educators with tools and resources to

use in a makerspace, including print resources, project ideas, student challenges, and tutorials.

National Electrical Contractors Association
3 Bethesda Metro Center, Suite 1100
Bethesda, MD 20814
(301) 657-4500
Website: https://www.necanet.org
Facebook: @NECANET
Twitter: @necanet
Instagram: @neca_net
This association of electrical contractors provides support to businesses and shares the latest industry news.

FOR FURTHER READING

Bailey, R. J. *Electrical Engineer.* Minneapolis, MN: Jump!, 2017.

Brejcha, Lacy. *Makerspaces in School: A Month-by-Month Schoolwide Model for Building Meaningful Maker-spaces.* Waco, TX: Prufrock Press, 2018.

Chatterton, Crystal. *Awesome Science Experiments for Kids: 100+ Fun STEM/STEAM Projects and Why They Work.* Emeryville, CA: Rockridge Press, 2018.

Fleming, Laura. *The Kickstart Guide to Making GREAT Mak-erspaces.* Thousand Oaks, CA: Corwin, 2017.

Fleming, Laura. *Worlds of Making: Best Practices for Estab-lishing a Makerspace for Your School.* Thousand Oaks, CA: Corwin, 2015.

Gardner, Robert, and Joshua Conklin. *Experiments for Future Engineers.* Berkeley Heights, NJ: Enslow Publish-ing, 2016.

Graves, Colleen, and Aaron Graves. *The Big Book of Makerspace Projects: Inspiring Makers to Experiment, Create, and Learn.* New York, NY: McGraw-Hill Educa-tion, 2016.

Institute for Career Research. *Career as an Electrician: Electrical Contractor.* Scotts Valley, CA: CreateSpace Independent Publishing Platform, 2015.

Provenzano, Nicholas. *Your Starter Guide to Makerspaces.* Blend Education, 2016.

Sandall, Barbara R. *Using STEM to Investigate Issues in Alternative Energy,* Grades 6–8. Greensboro, NC: Mark Twain Media, 2011.

BIBLIOGRAPHY

Balance Careers. "Do You Have What It Takes to Be an Electrician?" Retrieved October 18, 2018. https://www.thebalancecareers.com/quiz-do-you-have-what-it-takes-to-be-an-electrician-4100321.

Best College Reviews. "The 50 Best Pre-college Summer Science Programs for High School Students." Retrieved September 20, 2018. https://www.bestcollegereviews.org/features/pre-college-summer-science-programs-high-school-students.

BestColleges.com. "Best Online Bachelor's in Electrical Engineering Programs." Retrieved October 18, 2018. https://www.bestcolleges.com/features/top-online-electrical-engineering-programs.

Bureau of Labor Statistics. "Electrical and Electronics Engineers." Retrieved October 18, 2018. https://www.bls.gov/ooh/architecture-and-engineering/electrical-and-electronics-engineers.htm.

Burke, John J. *Makerspaces: A Practical Guide for Librarians.* Lanham, MD: Rowman & Littlefield Publishers, 2014.

Crawford, Matthew B. *Shop Class as Soulcraft.* New York, NY: Penguin Books, 2010.

Gonzalez, Jennifer. "What Is the Point of a Makerspace?" *Cult of Pedagogy* (blog), May 20, 2018. https://www.cultofpedagogy.com/makerspace.

Hardenbrook, Joe. "Making Sense of Makerspaces: Academic Library Staff Respond to a Makerspace." Retrieved September 20, 2018. https://mrlibrarydude.wordpress.com/2017/12/04/making-sense-of-makerspaces-academic-library-staff-response-to-a-makerspace.

LeBrett, Becky. "Want to Create a Budget-Friendly Makerspace in the New Year? Think, Plan, and Organize." *Make:*, January 12, 2018. https://makezine .com/2018/01/12/want-create-budget-friendly -makerspace-new-year-think-plan-organize.

Lynch, Matthew. "10 Reasons to Create Makerspaces in Your School." Tech Edvocate, January 21, 2017. https://www.thetechedvocate.org/10-reasons-to -create-makerspaces-in-your-school.

Lynch, Matthew. "Why Makerspaces Are the Key to Innovation." Tech Edvocate, January 19, 2017. https://www.thetechedvocate.org/why-makerspaces -are-the-key-to-innovation.

Makerspaces.com. "What Is a Makerspace?" Retrieved September 20, 2018. https://www.makerspaces.com /what-is-a-makerspace.

Merriam-Webster. "Electronics." Retrieved October 18, 2018. https://www.merriam-webster.com/dictionary/electronics.

New Media Consortium. *NMC Horizon Report > 2015 K–12 Edition*. Retrieved September 20, 2018. https://www.nmc.org/publication/nmc-horizon-report -2015-k-12-edition.

Open Education Database. "A Librarian's Guide to Makerspaces: 16 Resources." Retrieved September 20, 2018. https://oedb.org/ilibrarian/a-librarians -guide-to-makerspaces.

Schulman, Kori. "White House Hangout: The Maker Movement." White House: President Barack Obama, March 27, 2013. https://obamawhitehouse.archives .gov/blog/2013/03/27/white-house-hangout -maker-movement.

Swan, Noelle. "The 'Maker Movement' Creates D.I.Y. Revolution." *Christian Science Monitor*, July 6, 2014. https://www.csmonitor.com/Technology/2014/0706/The-maker-movement-creates-D.I.Y.-revolution.

TeachThought Staff. "It's Vital Your Makerspace Reflects the Culture of Your School." TeachThought, November 15, 2015. https://www.teachthought.com/learning/its-vital-your-makerspace-reflects-the-culture-of-your-school.

Trade Schools, Colleges and Universities. "What Is Technology If Not Change?" Retrieved September 20, 2018. https://www.trade-schools.net/articles/electronics-jobs.asp.

U.S. News & World Report. "Best Electrical/Electronic/Communications Engineering Programs." Retrieved October 18, 2018. https://www.usnews.com/best-graduate-schools/top-engineering-schools/electrical-engineering-rankings.

ABOUT THE AUTHOR

Tracy Brown Hamilton is a writer and journalist who has written many books on a variety of topics, including career guides, biographies, and health and media-related subjects. She lives in the Netherlands with her husband and three children.

PHOTO CREDITS